The Data Driven Entrepreneur

Making Informed Decisions for Business Growth

Basil U.

COPYRIGHT PAGE

All right reserved. No part of this publication may be published in any means or by any form, either by photocopying, scanning or otherwise without any prior written permission from the copyright holder.

Copyright © 2024 Basil U.

About the Author

Basil is a software engineer based in Dubai, United Arab Emirate, he has worked as a Developer for over 8 years and has been building dynamic web applications, for personal and for companies world wide.

In the time past his experience has helped different kinds of companies ranging from startups to large scale enterprises. He is also vast in knowledge with CLoud Computation, Mobile Application Development, AI Integration, API Integration and Databases.

I am grateful to my family who has been a huge support to me since I started writing this book. Thanks to my wife Onyi and children for their endless support.

Content

Chapter One
Introduction
Chapter Two
Understanding Data-Driven Decision-Making
Chapter Three
Collecting and Analyzing Data
Chapter Four
Integrating Data into Business Strategy
Chapter Five
Building a Data-Driven Culture
Chapter Six
Case Studies and Success Stories
Chapter Seven
Challenges and Ethical Considerations
Chapter Eight
Implementing Data-Driven Decisions
Chapter Nine
The Future of Data-Driven Decision-Making
Chapter Ten
Conclusion

Chapter One

Introduction

In the fast-paced and ever-evolving world of modern business, data has emerged as a critical asset that can make or break a company's success. As entrepreneurs navigate the complexities of today's marketplace, the ability to harness and interpret data has become indispensable. This shift towards data-driven decision-making is not just a trend; it's a fundamental transformation in how businesses operate, innovate, and grow. In this introduction, we will explore the importance of data in modern business, how data-driven decisions can enhance business outcomes, and provide an overview of what this book will cover.

The Importance of Data in Modern Business

In the digital age, data is often referred to as the "new oil," a valuable resource that fuels innovation, drives strategy, and provides a competitive edge. Unlike traditional resources, however, data is virtually limitless and can be continuously generated, collected, and analyzed. This wealth of information, when properly leveraged, can offer deep insights into customer behavior, market trends, operational efficiencies, and much more.

1. Data as a Competitive Advantage

One of the primary reasons data is so crucial in modern business is its ability to provide a competitive advantage. Companies that can effectively gather, analyze, and act on data are often able to outmaneuver their competitors. This competitive edge manifests in various ways:

- **Personalized Customer Experiences:** Businesses that understand their customers through data can tailor their products, services, and marketing efforts to meet individual needs and preferences. This personalization fosters customer loyalty and can significantly boost sales.
- **Market Trend Analysis:** Data allows businesses to identify and capitalize on emerging trends before

their competitors. By staying ahead of the curve, companies can introduce new products, adjust strategies, and position themselves as leaders in their industries.

- **Operational Efficiency:** Data-driven insights can reveal inefficiencies in business processes, enabling companies to optimize operations, reduce costs, and improve overall productivity.

2. The Evolution of Data-Driven Business

The concept of using data to inform business decisions is not new. However, the scale, speed, and sophistication with which data is now utilized have transformed the landscape. Historically, businesses relied on intuition, experience, and limited data sets to make decisions. While these methods still have their place, they are increasingly being supplemented—and often replaced—by data-driven approaches.

Several factors have contributed to this evolution:

- **Technological Advancements:** The rise of big data, cloud computing, artificial intelligence (AI), and machine learning has made it easier and more cost-effective for businesses of all sizes to collect, store, and analyze vast amounts of data.
- **Digital Transformation:** As businesses undergo digital transformation, they generate more data than ever before. From online transactions to social media interactions, every touchpoint creates data that can be mined for insights.
- **Increased Competition:** In today's globalized economy, competition is fiercer than ever. Businesses must leverage every available resource to stay competitive, and data has become a key weapon in this battle.

3. Data-Driven Cultures and Decision-Making

For businesses to truly benefit from data, they must cultivate a data-driven culture. This involves more than just investing in technology; it requires a shift in mindset across the organization. In a data-driven culture:

- **Decisions Are Informed by Data:** Leaders and employees at all levels use data to inform their decisions, rather than relying solely on gut feelings or anecdotal evidence.
- **Data Literacy Is Encouraged:** Employees are trained to understand and interpret data, making it accessible and useful to everyone, not just data scientists or analysts.
- **Data Is Integrated into Daily Operations:** Data is not siloed but is integrated into all aspects of the business, from marketing and sales to operations and finance.

By fostering a data-driven culture, businesses can ensure that data is consistently leveraged to improve decision-making and drive better outcomes.

How Data-Driven Decisions Can Enhance Business Outcomes

The impact of data-driven decision-making on business outcomes is profound. When businesses make decisions based on data, they are more likely to achieve their goals, mitigate risks, and create value. Let's explore some of the key ways in which data-driven decisions can enhance business outcomes:

1. Improved Accuracy and Objectivity

One of the most significant advantages of data-driven decision-making is the improvement in accuracy and objectivity. Traditional decision-making processes often involve a degree of subjectivity, where personal biases, assumptions, and emotions can influence outcomes. Data-driven decisions, on the other hand, rely on factual information and statistical analysis, which reduces the risk of errors and bias.

- **Example:** A retail company uses historical sales data to forecast demand for its products during the holiday season. By analyzing trends and patterns, the company can make accurate inventory decisions, reducing the risk of stockouts or overstocking.

2. Enhanced Agility and Responsiveness

In today's fast-paced business environment, agility is crucial. Businesses need to be able to respond quickly to changes in the market, customer behavior, and competitive landscape. Data-driven decision-making enables businesses to be more agile and responsive by providing real-time insights and enabling rapid adjustments to strategies and operations.

- **Example:** An e-commerce company monitors customer behavior in real-time, such as which products are being viewed or added to carts. If a particular product is trending, the company can quickly adjust its marketing efforts to capitalize on the trend.

3. Better Resource Allocation

Effective resource allocation is critical to maximizing profitability and growth. Data-driven decision-making helps businesses allocate resources more efficiently by identifying which areas of the business are generating the most value and which areas may require improvement.

- **Example:** A manufacturing company uses data analytics to identify which production lines are most efficient and which are underperforming. The company can then allocate resources, such as labor and capital, to optimize production and reduce waste.

4. Increased Customer Satisfaction and Retention

Understanding customer needs and preferences is essential for building strong relationships and driving customer loyalty. Data-driven decision-making allows businesses to gain deep insights into customer behavior, preferences, and pain points, enabling them to deliver personalized experiences that increase satisfaction and retention.

- **Example:** A subscription-based service uses customer data to identify which features are most valued by its users. By focusing on enhancing these features and addressing any issues, the company can improve customer satisfaction and reduce churn rates.

5. Risk Mitigation and Strategic Planning

Data-driven decision-making is also a powerful tool for risk mitigation and strategic planning. By analyzing data, businesses can identify potential risks, forecast future scenarios, and develop strategies to mitigate those risks and capitalize on opportunities.

- **Example:** A financial services company uses data analytics to assess the risk of default for loan applicants. By analyzing factors such as credit history, income, and spending behavior, the company can make more informed lending decisions and reduce the risk of defaults.

6. Innovation and Growth

Data-driven decision-making is a catalyst for innovation and growth. By analyzing data, businesses can identify new opportunities, develop innovative products and services, and expand into new markets.

- **Example:** A tech startup uses data analytics to identify gaps in the market and develop a new product that addresses an unmet need. By continuously analyzing customer feedback and usage data, the startup can refine the product and drive growth.

Overview of What the Book Will Cover

This book is designed to be a comprehensive guide for entrepreneurs who want to harness the power of data to make smarter, more informed decisions. Whether you are just starting your entrepreneurial journey or are looking to take your existing business to the next level, this book will provide you with the knowledge, tools, and strategies you need to succeed in the data-driven world of modern business.

Understanding Data-Driven Decision-Making

- This chapter will introduce you to the concept of data-driven decision-making, explaining what it is, why it matters, and how it differs from traditional decision-making approaches. You'll learn about the key components of data-driven decision-making and how it can be applied across various aspects of your business.

Collecting and Analyzing Data

- In this chapter, we will explore the different types of data that entrepreneurs can collect, including quantitative and qualitative data. We'll discuss the key sources of data for businesses, such as customer data, market trends, and sales figures. You'll also learn about the tools and technologies available for data collection and analysis, as well as techniques for data visualization.

Integrating Data into Business Strategy

- This chapter will focus on how to align data insights with your business goals. You'll learn how to develop data-driven strategies for key business functions, including marketing, operations, and product development. We'll also explore the role of data in identifying opportunities and risks, and how to use data to make informed strategic decisions.

Building a Data-Driven Culture

- Creating a data-driven culture within your organization is essential for maximizing the value of data. In this chapter, we'll discuss how to foster a data-driven mindset among your team, encourage data literacy, and integrate data into daily operations. You'll also learn about the challenges of building a data-driven culture and how to overcome them.

Case Studies and Success Stories

- This chapter will provide real-world examples of successful entrepreneurs who have leveraged data to grow their businesses. We'll explore case studies from various industries, highlighting the strategies and techniques that have led to success. You'll also learn from the mistakes and failures of others, gaining valuable insights into what works—and what doesn't—when it comes to data-driven decision-making.

Challenges and Ethical Considerations

- Data-driven decision-making comes with its own set of challenges and ethical considerations. In this chapter, we'll discuss common challenges such as data quality, analysis paralysis, and resistance to change. We'll also explore the ethical implications of data use, including privacy concerns, data bias, and the responsible use of data.

Implementing Data-Driven Decisions

- This chapter will provide a step-by-step guide to implementing data-driven decisions in your business. You'll learn how to move from data collection to execution, monitor and evaluate the outcomes of your decisions, and iterate and improve based on results. We'll also discuss the importance of agility and continuous improvement in the data-driven decision-making process.

The Future of Data-Driven Decision-Making

- The final chapter will look ahead to the future of data-driven decision-making, exploring emerging trends in data analytics, artificial intelligence, and machine learning. You'll learn how these technologies are shaping the future of business and how you can prepare your business to thrive in a data-driven world.

- The conclusion will recap the key points covered in the book and provide encouragement for entrepreneurs to embrace data-driven decision-making as a core component of their business strategy. We'll also provide additional resources for further learning and next steps for implementing the concepts discussed in the book.

By the end of this book, you will have a deep understanding of data-driven decision-making and the tools and strategies needed to apply it in your business. You'll be equipped to make smarter, more informed decisions that drive growth, innovation, and success in today's competitive marketplace. Whether you're looking to improve your existing business or launch a new venture, this book will serve as your guide to navigating the data-driven world of modern entrepreneurship.

Chapter Two

Understanding Data-Driven Decision-Making

In today's rapidly evolving business environment, the ability to make informed, data-driven decisions is a crucial skill for entrepreneurs. Whether you're a startup founder, a small business owner, or a seasoned executive, understanding how to leverage data effectively can be the difference between success and failure. In this section, we'll explore the concept of data-driven decision-making, how it contrasts with intuition-based decisions, and the numerous benefits that come from making decisions rooted in data.

What is Data-Driven Decision-Making?

Data-driven decision-making refers to the process of making choices based on data analysis rather than intuition, gut feeling, or personal experience alone. It involves collecting, analyzing, and interpreting data to guide business decisions, from minor operational tweaks to major strategic shifts. By relying on data, entrepreneurs can remove much of the guesswork from decision-making, leading to more accurate and effective outcomes.

At its core, data-driven decision-making is about transforming raw data into actionable insights. This transformation process involves several key steps:

1. **Data Collection**: Gathering relevant data from various sources. This could include sales figures, customer feedback, market research, web analytics, social media metrics, and more.
2. **Data Processing and Analysis**: Once collected, data must be processed and analyzed to uncover trends, patterns, and correlations. This often involves the use of statistical tools, data visualization techniques, and machine learning algorithms.
3. **Data Interpretation**: After analyzing the data, the next step is to interpret the results. This involves understanding what the data is telling you about

your business, your customers, and the market at large.

4. **Decision Making:** Finally, the insights gained from data interpretation are used to inform decision-making. Whether you're launching a new product, tweaking your marketing strategy, or optimizing your supply chain, data-driven decisions are grounded in evidence rather than speculation.

A key aspect of data-driven decision-making is its iterative nature. It's not a one-time process but an ongoing cycle of collecting data, analyzing it, making decisions, and then collecting more data to assess the impact of those decisions. This continuous feedback loop allows entrepreneurs to refine their strategies over time, leading to more efficient and effective business operations.

The Difference Between Intuition-Based and Data-Driven Decisions

For many entrepreneurs, intuition has been the cornerstone of their decision-making process. After all, intuition is often seen as a valuable asset in business—a combination of experience, knowledge, and instinct that guides leaders in uncertain situations. However, while intuition can be powerful, it has its limitations, especially in today's data-rich environment.

1. Basis of Decision-Making

- **Intuition-Based Decisions:** These decisions are primarily based on personal experience, gut feelings, and instincts. Entrepreneurs may rely on their past successes or failures, their understanding of the industry, and their perception of the market when making these decisions.
- **Data-Driven Decisions:** In contrast, data-driven decisions are based on empirical evidence. Entrepreneurs use data analysis to identify

patterns, trends, and correlations, which then inform their choices. This approach reduces the reliance on subjective judgment and provides a more objective basis for decision-making.

2. **Accuracy and Reliability**

- **Intuition-Based Decisions:** While intuition can sometimes lead to successful outcomes, it is not always reliable. Intuition is susceptible to biases, such as confirmation bias (favoring information that confirms existing beliefs) and availability bias (relying on recent or easily recalled information). These biases can lead to flawed decision-making, especially in complex or unfamiliar situations.
- **Data-Driven Decisions:** By grounding decisions in data, entrepreneurs can reduce the influence of biases and improve the accuracy and reliability of their choices. Data provides a factual basis for decision-making, which can be especially valuable in situations where the stakes are high or where the entrepreneur lacks prior experience.

3. Scalability and Adaptability

- **Intuition-Based Decisions:** Intuition can be effective in small-scale or familiar contexts, where the entrepreneur has a deep understanding of the business and its environment. However, as a business grows and becomes more complex, relying solely on intuition can become increasingly risky.
- **Data-Driven Decisions:** Data-driven decision-making is inherently scalable. As a business expands, the volume and complexity of data it generates also increase. By leveraging data analytics tools and techniques, entrepreneurs can continue to make informed decisions even as their business evolves and the market changes.

4. Risk Management

- **Intuition-Based Decisions:** Intuition can be useful in high-pressure situations where quick decisions are needed, but it can also increase the risk of errors. Without data to back up decisions, entrepreneurs may be more prone to making costly mistakes.

- **Data-Driven Decisions:** Data-driven decisions involve a more systematic and analytical approach, which can help mitigate risks. By analyzing historical data, entrepreneurs can identify potential pitfalls and take proactive measures to avoid them. Additionally, data-driven decisions often involve scenario analysis, allowing entrepreneurs to assess the potential outcomes of different choices before committing to a course of action.

5. Innovation and Creativity

- **Intuition-Based Decisions:** Intuition is often associated with creativity and innovation, as it allows entrepreneurs to think outside the box and take bold risks. Some of the most successful entrepreneurs are known for their intuitive leaps and unconventional thinking.

- **Data-Driven Decisions:** While data-driven decision-making is more structured and analytical, it doesn't necessarily stifle creativity. In fact, data can be a powerful tool for innovation. By uncovering hidden trends and patterns, data can inspire new ideas and opportunities that entrepreneurs may not have considered otherwise. The key is to strike a balance between intuition and data, using each to complement the other.

Benefits of Making Decisions Based on Data

Adopting a data-driven approach to decision-making offers numerous benefits, particularly for entrepreneurs who are navigating the uncertainties and challenges of building and growing a business. Here are some of the key advantages:

1. **Increased Accuracy and Precision**

- **Improved Forecasting:** Data-driven decisions are based on concrete evidence, which leads to more accurate forecasts and projections. For example, by analyzing historical sales data, an entrepreneur can more accurately predict future demand, enabling better inventory management and resource allocation.

- **Targeted Marketing:** Data allows for highly targeted marketing strategies. By analyzing customer data, entrepreneurs can segment their audience more effectively, tailoring marketing messages to specific demographics, behaviors, and preferences. This increases the likelihood of conversions and reduces marketing spend wastage.

2. Enhanced Efficiency and Productivity

- **Resource Optimization:** Data-driven decision-making helps entrepreneurs allocate resources more efficiently. For instance, by analyzing operational data, a business owner can identify bottlenecks in the production process and implement changes to improve productivity.

- **Process Improvement:** Data analysis can reveal inefficiencies in business processes, enabling entrepreneurs to streamline operations and reduce costs. Continuous monitoring and analysis also allow for ongoing process improvements, driving long-term efficiency gains.

3. **Better Risk Management**

- **Identifying Trends and Patterns:** One of the key benefits of data-driven decision-making is the ability to identify trends and patterns that may not be immediately obvious. By recognizing these trends early, entrepreneurs can take proactive steps to mitigate risks and capitalize on opportunities.
- **Scenario Planning:** Data-driven decisions often involve scenario planning, where different potential outcomes are modeled and analyzed. This approach allows entrepreneurs to assess the risks and benefits of various options before

making a final decision, reducing the likelihood of unexpected negative outcomes.

4. Improved Customer Understanding

- **Customer Insights:** Data provides valuable insights into customer behavior, preferences, and needs. By analyzing customer data, entrepreneurs can gain a deeper understanding of their target audience, allowing them to tailor their products, services, and marketing efforts to better meet customer expectations.

- **Personalization:** Data-driven decision-making enables businesses to deliver personalized experiences to their customers. For example, by analyzing purchase history and browsing behavior, an online retailer can recommend products that are most likely to appeal to individual customers, increasing the chances of a sale.

5. Greater Agility and Responsiveness

- **Real-Time Decision-Making:** With the right tools and infrastructure, data can be collected and analyzed in real time, enabling entrepreneurs to make decisions quickly and respond to changes in the market as they happen. This agility is crucial in today's fast-paced business environment, where the ability to pivot quickly can be a competitive advantage.

- **Continuous Improvement:** Data-driven decision-making supports a culture of continuous improvement. By regularly analyzing data and measuring the impact of decisions, entrepreneurs can iterate on their strategies and make ongoing adjustments to optimize performance.

6. Stronger Competitive Advantage

- **Informed Strategy:** Entrepreneurs who base their decisions on data are better equipped to develop informed strategies that give them a competitive edge. By leveraging data to understand market trends, customer needs, and competitor actions, businesses can position themselves more effectively in the marketplace.

- **Innovation Opportunities:** Data can also be a source of innovation. By analyzing industry data, customer feedback, and market trends, entrepreneurs can identify unmet needs and emerging opportunities, leading to the development of new products, services, or business models.

7. Increased Accountability and Transparency

- **Objective Decision-Making:** Data-driven decision-making promotes accountability by providing an objective basis for decisions. This transparency can help build trust within the organization and with external stakeholders, as decisions are based on evidence rather than personal biases or opinions.
- **Performance Measurement:** Data-driven decisions are easier to measure and evaluate.

Entrepreneurs can track key performance indicators (KPIs) and other metrics to assess the impact of their decisions, making it easier to hold themselves and their teams accountable for results.

8. Alignment with Business Goals

- **Strategic Alignment:** Data-driven decision-making ensures that decisions are aligned with the overall business strategy. By setting clear goals and using data to measure progress, entrepreneurs can ensure that their decisions contribute to the achievement of those goals.
- **Resource Alignment:** Data-driven decisions also help align resources with business priorities. By analyzing data on resource utilization, entrepreneurs can ensure that their time, money, and effort are focused on the areas that will have the greatest impact on their business.

9. Enhanced Long-Term Planning

- **Strategic Forecasting:** Data-driven decision-making supports long-term planning by providing insights into future trends and potential challenges. Entrepreneurs can use data to develop strategic forecasts and prepare for different scenarios, ensuring that their business is well-positioned for future success.
- **Sustainable Growth:** By making informed decisions based on data, entrepreneurs can drive sustainable growth. Data-driven strategies are more likely to lead to steady, manageable growth, as they are grounded in evidence rather than speculation or overly optimistic assumptions.

Understanding data-driven decision-making is essential for entrepreneurs who want to thrive in today's competitive business landscape. By leveraging data, entrepreneurs can make more accurate, efficient, and strategic decisions that drive growth, mitigate risks, and enhance customer satisfaction. While intuition and experience will always play a role in business, the ability to incorporate data into decision-making processes is becoming increasingly important. As data analytics tools and technologies continue to evolve, the opportunities for data-driven decision-making will only expand, offering entrepreneurs new ways to innovate, compete, and succeed.

This chapter has provided an overview of what data-driven decision-making is, how it compares to intuition-based decision-making, and the many benefits it offers. As you continue to explore the world of data-driven entrepreneurship, remember that the key to success is not just collecting data but using it effectively to inform your decisions and drive your business forward.

Chapter Three

Collecting and Analyzing Data

In the realm of entrepreneurship, data is an invaluable asset that can drive decision-making and fuel business growth. Understanding how to effectively collect and analyze data is critical for making informed choices that align with your strategic goals. This section delves into the different types of data, key sources, essential tools and technologies, and data visualization techniques to help you leverage data for business success.

Types of Data: Quantitative vs. Qualitative

1. Quantitative Data

Quantitative data refers to numerical information that can be measured and analyzed statistically. It provides a clear, objective basis for making decisions and assessing performance.

- Characteristics:
    - **Numerical:** Quantitative data is expressed in numbers, making it ideal for statistical analysis.
    - **Objective:** This data type reduces subjectivity, providing a concrete basis for decisions.
    - **Easily Measurable:** Quantitative data can be collected through various methods such as surveys, sales reports, and financial statements.
- Examples:
    - **Sales Figures:** Data on the number of units sold, revenue generated, and average order value.
    - **Website Metrics:** Statistics such as page views, bounce rates, and conversion rates.
    - **Market Research:** Data on market share, customer demographics, and industry growth rates.

2. Qualitative Data

Qualitative data is descriptive and conceptual. It provides deeper insights into customer behaviors, motivations, and experiences that are not easily captured by numerical data alone.

- Characteristics:
    - **Descriptive:** Focuses on characteristics, attributes, and qualities.
    - **Subjective:** Reflects personal opinions and interpretations.
    - **Rich in Detail:** Provides context and understanding that can complement quantitative data.
- Examples:
    - **Customer Feedback:** Insights from surveys, interviews, and reviews that describe customer experiences and opinions.
    - **Market Trends:** Observations about emerging trends and shifts in consumer behavior.

- **Employee Insights:** Feedback from staff about operational challenges and opportunities.

Key Sources of Data for Entrepreneurs

Entrepreneurs have access to a wide range of data sources that can provide valuable insights into their business and market environment. Understanding these sources helps in making informed decisions that drive growth and success.

1. Customer Data

- **Definition:** Information collected from interactions with customers, including purchase history, preferences, and behavior.
- **Importance:** Helps in understanding customer needs, predicting trends, and personalizing marketing efforts.
- **Sources:**
    - **CRM Systems:** Track customer interactions, sales, and service records.

- **Surveys and Feedback:** Collect direct input from customers about their experiences and satisfaction.
- **Website Analytics:** Monitor user behavior on your site, including browsing patterns and conversion rates.

2. Market Trends

- **Definition:** Insights into the broader market environment, including industry developments, competitor activities, and consumer behavior.
- **Importance:** Enables businesses to anticipate changes, identify opportunities, and stay competitive.
- **Sources:**
  - **Industry Reports:** Published by market research firms and industry associations.
  - **Competitor Analysis:** Tracking competitors' activities, product launches, and market positioning.

- **Social Media Trends:** Monitoring discussions, hashtags, and sentiment on platforms like Twitter, Facebook, and LinkedIn.

3. Sales Figures

- **Definition:** Data related to the revenue generated from sales, including transaction volume and profitability.
- **Importance:** Essential for assessing financial performance, evaluating sales strategies, and forecasting future revenue.
- **Sources:**
    - **Point-of-Sale (POS) Systems:** Record transactions and generate sales reports.
    - **Financial Statements:** Provide a comprehensive view of revenue, expenses, and profitability.
    - **E-commerce Platforms:** Track online sales, customer orders, and product performance.

4. Operational Data

- **Definition:** Information related to business operations, including supply chain, inventory, and production.
- **Importance:** Helps in optimizing processes, reducing costs, and improving efficiency.
- **Sources:**
  - **Inventory Management Systems:** Track stock levels, turnover rates, and supply chain logistics.
  - **Production Reports:** Monitor manufacturing output, quality control, and operational efficiency.
  - **Supplier Data:** Assess supplier performance, delivery times, and cost.

Tools and Technologies for Data Collection and Analysis

Utilizing the right tools and technologies is crucial for efficiently collecting and analyzing data. These tools help in gathering accurate information, performing detailed analysis, and making data-driven decisions.

1. Data Collection Tools

   - Surveys and Forms:
     - **Examples:** Google Forms, SurveyMonkey, Typeform.
     - **Features:** Allows for the creation of customized surveys to gather customer feedback, opinions, and preferences.
     - **Benefits:** Easy to use and distribute, with features for data aggregation and analysis.
   - Customer Relationship Management (CRM) Systems:
     - **Examples:** Salesforce, HubSpot, Zoho CRM.
     - **Features:** Manages customer interactions, tracks sales activities, and stores customer data.
     - **Benefits:** Centralizes customer information, provides insights into customer behavior, and supports personalized marketing.
   - Analytics Platforms:
     - **Examples:** Google Analytics, Adobe Analytics.

- **Features:** Tracks website traffic, user behavior, and conversion metrics.
- **Benefits:** Provides detailed reports on site performance, visitor demographics, and marketing effectiveness.

2. Data Analysis Tools

- **Spreadsheet Software:**
    - **Examples:** Microsoft Excel, Google Sheets.
    - **Features:** Offers data organization, analysis, and visualization capabilities.
    - **Benefits:** Versatile tool for performing statistical analysis, creating charts, and managing datasets.
- **Business Intelligence (BI) Tools:**
    - **Examples:** Tableau, Power BI, Looker.
    - **Features:** Provides advanced data analysis, visualization, and reporting capabilities.
    - **Benefits:** Facilitates in-depth analysis, interactive dashboards, and real-time data insights.

- **Statistical Analysis Software:**
    - **Examples:** SPSS, R, SAS.
    - **Features:** Offers advanced statistical analysis, data modeling, and hypothesis testing.
    - **Benefits:** Enables sophisticated data analysis, including regression, factor analysis, and predictive modeling.

3. Data Integration Tools

- **Data Warehousing Solutions:**
    - **Examples:** Amazon Redshift, Google BigQuery.
    - **Features:** Centralizes data from various sources into a unified repository.
    - **Benefits:** Facilitates comprehensive analysis by combining data from multiple systems and platforms.
- **ETL (Extract, Transform, Load) Tools:**
    - **Examples:** Talend, Apache Nifi, Informatica.

- **Features:** Extracts data from different sources, transforms it into a usable format, and loads it into a data warehouse.
- **Benefits:** Automates data integration and ensures data consistency across systems.

Data Visualization Techniques to Simplify Complex Data

Data visualization is essential for interpreting complex data and communicating insights effectively. By presenting data visually, you can identify patterns, trends, and outliers that might not be apparent from raw data alone.

1. Types of Data Visualizations

- Charts and Graphs:
    - **Bar Charts:** Compare quantities across different categories. Useful for showing sales performance or market share.
    - **Line Graphs:** Display trends over time. Ideal for tracking changes in revenue, website traffic, or customer behavior.

- **Pie Charts:** Show proportions and percentages. Effective for illustrating the distribution of market segments or revenue sources.

• **Tables:**
    - **Data Tables:** Present detailed data in rows and columns. Useful for displaying numerical data, such as sales figures or inventory levels.
    - **Pivot Tables:** Summarize and analyze large datasets. Helpful for aggregating sales data, customer information, or operational metrics.

• **Heatmaps:**
    - **Definition:** Visualize data density and intensity using color gradients.
    - **Usage:** Ideal for displaying website user interactions, customer activity, or sales performance by region.

- Dashboards:
  - **Definition:** Interactive displays that consolidate multiple visualizations into a single view.
  - **Usage:** Provide a comprehensive overview of key metrics and performance indicators. Useful for real-time monitoring and decision-making.

2. Best Practices for Data Visualization

- **Clarity:** Ensure that visualizations are easy to understand and interpret. Avoid clutter and focus on conveying key messages.
- **Consistency:** Use consistent colors, labels, and formats across visualizations to facilitate comparison and understanding.
- **Context:** Provide context and explanations for visualizations to help viewers understand the data and its implications.

- **Interactivity:** Incorporate interactive elements, such as filters and drill-down options, to allow users to explore data in more detail.

Collecting and analyzing data is a foundational aspect of data-driven decision-making. By understanding the different types of data, utilizing key sources, employing effective tools and technologies, and mastering data visualization techniques, entrepreneurs can make informed decisions that drive business success. Embracing these practices will enable you to leverage data as a powerful asset, optimize your strategies, and achieve your business goals with confidence.

Chapter Four

Integrating Data into Business Strategy

In today's competitive landscape, integrating data into your business strategy is not just an option—it's essential. Data-driven decision-making empowers entrepreneurs to make informed choices that align with their business goals, uncover opportunities, mitigate risks, and drive sustainable growth. This section explores how to align data insights with business goals, provides examples of data-driven strategies across various business functions, and highlights the role of data in identifying opportunities and risks.

Aligning Data Insights with Business Goals

1. Setting Clear Objectives

The foundation of aligning data with business strategy is to have clear and well-defined objectives. These objectives should be Specific, Measurable, Achievable, Relevant, and Time-bound (SMART). By setting clear goals, you create a roadmap for what you want to achieve, which guides the data collection and analysis process.

- **Specific:** Define precisely what you want to achieve. For instance, instead of aiming to "increase sales," set a goal to "increase online sales by 20% in the next six months."
- **Measurable:** Establish metrics to track progress. This might include sales figures, customer acquisition rates, or website traffic.
- **Achievable:** Ensure that the goals are realistic given your resources and market conditions.
- **Relevant:** Align goals with your overall business strategy and vision.
- **Time-bound:** Set deadlines to create urgency and focus.

2. Identifying Key Performance Indicators (KPIs)

KPIs are quantifiable measures that help track progress towards your business objectives. Choosing the right KPIs involves understanding what metrics will provide insights into the success of your strategies. Common KPIs for various business functions include:

- **Sales and Revenue:** Total revenue, average order value, sales growth rate.
- **Marketing:** Customer acquisition cost, conversion rate, return on investment (ROI) for marketing campaigns.
- **Operations:** Inventory turnover, order fulfillment time, production costs.
- **Customer Service:** Customer satisfaction score, net promoter score (NPS), customer retention rate.

By focusing on these KPIs, you can ensure that the data you collect and analyze is directly tied to your business goals.

3. Data Collection and Analysis

Once you've established your objectives and KPIs, the next step is to collect and analyze data. This involves gathering relevant data from various sources and using analytical tools to derive insights. Here's how you can approach this:

- **Data Collection:** Utilize tools and technologies to gather data from multiple sources, including customer interactions, sales transactions, website analytics, and market research. Ensure data quality by focusing on accuracy, completeness, and timeliness.
- **Data Analysis:** Employ statistical methods and analytical tools to interpret the data. Look for trends, patterns, and correlations that provide insights into your business performance. Data visualization tools, such as charts and graphs, can help present complex data in an understandable format.

4. Translating Insights into Action

Data insights must be translated into actionable strategies. This involves interpreting the findings and making informed decisions that align with your business goals. For instance:

- **If Data Shows Low Customer Retention:** Implement loyalty programs or improve customer service to enhance retention.
- **If Sales Data Indicates Seasonal Trends:** Adjust inventory and marketing strategies to capitalize on peak periods.
- **If Website Analytics Reveal High Bounce Rates:** Optimize website design and content to improve user experience.

By aligning data insights with strategic actions, you can ensure that your decisions are driven by evidence rather than intuition.

Examples of Data-Driven Strategies

1. Marketing

Data-driven marketing strategies rely on analytics to optimize campaigns and target the right audience. Here are some examples:

- **Personalized Marketing:** Use customer data to create personalized marketing messages and offers. For example, an e-commerce company might use purchase history to recommend products to customers based on their past behavior.

- **A/B Testing:** Test different versions of marketing materials (emails, ads, landing pages) to determine which performs better. By analyzing performance metrics, you can refine your marketing approach for better results.

- **Customer Segmentation:** Analyze customer data to segment your audience based on demographics, behavior, and preferences. Tailor marketing campaigns to each segment to increase engagement and conversion rates.

2. Operations

Data-driven operations strategies focus on improving efficiency and reducing costs. Examples include:

- **Supply Chain Optimization:** Use data to forecast demand and optimize inventory levels. By analyzing historical sales data and market trends, businesses can reduce excess inventory and avoid stockouts.

- **Process Improvement:** Analyze operational data to identify bottlenecks and inefficiencies in production or service delivery. Implement process improvements based on data insights to enhance productivity and reduce costs.
- **Performance Monitoring:** Track operational metrics to monitor performance and make data-driven adjustments. For instance, monitoring delivery times can help identify areas for improvement in logistics and distribution.

3. Product Development

Data-driven product development involves using insights to create products that meet customer needs and preferences. Examples include:

- **Customer Feedback Analysis:** Collect and analyze customer feedback to understand pain points and desires. Use this data to inform product design and feature development.

- **Market Research:** Conduct market research to identify trends and opportunities. For example, analyzing competitor products and market demand can guide the development of new product features or variations.
- **Usage Data:** Monitor how customers use your products to identify areas for enhancement. Data on usage patterns can inform updates and improvements that align with user needs.

The Role of Data in Identifying Opportunities and Risks

1. Identifying Opportunities

Data helps entrepreneurs uncover new opportunities by providing insights into market trends, customer behavior, and competitive dynamics. Here's how:

- **Market Trends:** Analyze market data to identify emerging trends and shifts in consumer preferences. This can help you anticipate changes and adapt your strategies accordingly.
- **Customer Insights:** Use customer data to identify unmet needs or gaps in the market. For example, if

data shows a growing interest in sustainable products, you might explore opportunities to develop eco-friendly offerings.

- **Competitive Analysis:** Monitor competitors' performance and strategies using data. Identify areas where you can differentiate your business or capitalize on competitor weaknesses.

2. Mitigating Risks

Data also plays a crucial role in risk management by helping you anticipate and mitigate potential issues. Examples include:

- **Financial Risks:** Analyze financial data to monitor cash flow, profit margins, and cost structures. Identify potential financial risks and take proactive measures to address them.
- **Operational Risks:** Use operational data to identify vulnerabilities in your processes. For instance, analyzing supply chain data can help you anticipate disruptions and develop contingency plans.

- **Market Risks:** Monitor market conditions and customer feedback to identify potential risks. For example, if data indicates a decline in customer satisfaction, address the issues to prevent negative impacts on your business.

3. Making Informed Decisions

Data-driven decision-making enables you to make informed choices that are based on evidence rather than guesswork. By leveraging data, you can:

- **Improve Accuracy:** Data provides a more accurate picture of your business environment, reducing the likelihood of errors in decision-making.
- **Enhance Objectivity:** Data-driven decisions are less influenced by personal biases or subjective opinions, leading to more objective outcomes.
- **Increase Agility:** With timely data insights, you can respond quickly to changing conditions and adjust your strategies accordingly.

Integrating data into your business strategy is a powerful approach for achieving your goals, optimizing operations, and driving growth. By setting clear objectives, identifying relevant KPIs, and utilizing data-driven strategies across marketing, operations, and product development, you can make informed decisions that align with your business goals. Additionally, leveraging data to identify opportunities and mitigate risks ensures that your decisions are grounded in evidence, enhancing your ability to navigate the complexities of the business landscape. Embracing a data-driven approach not only improves decision-making but also positions your business for long-term success.

Chapter Five

Building a Data-Driven Culture

Encouraging a Data-Driven Mindset Within Your Team

1. Leadership Commitment

- **Role of Leadership:** The commitment of senior leaders is vital for fostering a data-driven culture. Leaders must champion the use of data and model data-driven decision-making in their own actions.
- **Setting Expectations:** Communicate the importance of data in achieving business objectives. Ensure that data-driven decision-making is integrated into the company's vision and goals.

2. Creating a Data-Driven Vision

- **Defining the Vision:** Articulate a clear vision for how data will be used within the organization. This vision should align with the company's strategic objectives and demonstrate how data can drive business success.

- **Communicating the Vision:** Regularly communicate the vision to all team members. Use various channels such as meetings, newsletters, and internal communications to reinforce the message.

3. Promoting Data Literacy

- **Understanding Data's Value:** Educate employees about the benefits of data-driven decision-making. Highlight how data can improve efficiency, identify opportunities, and drive growth.
- **Encouraging Curiosity:** Foster a culture where questioning and exploring data is encouraged. Promote an environment where employees feel comfortable asking questions and seeking insights from data.

4. Celebrating Data Success Stories

- **Sharing Wins:** Regularly share success stories where data-driven decisions have led to positive outcomes. This can inspire other team members and demonstrate the practical benefits of using data.
- **Recognizing Achievements:** Acknowledge and reward employees who successfully use data to achieve business objectives. Recognition reinforces the value of data-driven efforts and motivates others to follow suit.

Training and Empowering Employees to Use Data Effectively

1. Providing Data Education and Training

- Tailored Training Programs: Develop training programs tailored to different roles within the organization. Ensure that training covers both the technical aspects of data tools and the strategic use of data.
- **Ongoing Learning:** Offer continuous learning opportunities to keep employees updated on new

tools, techniques, and best practices. Encourage participation in workshops, webinars, and industry conferences.

2. Implementing Data Tools and Platforms

- **Selecting Tools:** Choose data tools and platforms that are user-friendly and meet the needs of your organization. Ensure that the tools are accessible to employees at all levels.
- **Training on Tools:** Provide hands-on training on how to use data tools effectively. This includes data visualization tools, analytics platforms, and data management systems.

3. Encouraging Data-Driven Decision-Making

- **Integrating Data into Daily Operations:** Encourage employees to use data in their daily tasks and decision-making processes. Provide guidelines and support on how to incorporate data into routine activities.

- **Empowering Decision-Making:** Empower employees to make data-driven decisions within their areas of responsibility. Provide the necessary data and resources to enable informed decision-making.

4. Building Cross-Functional Teams

- **Collaborative Approach:** Promote collaboration between different departments to leverage diverse data perspectives. Cross-functional teams can provide more comprehensive insights and drive innovative solutions.
- **Sharing Best Practices:** Facilitate the sharing of data-driven practices and insights across teams. This can lead to more effective use of data and foster a culture of knowledge sharing.

Overcoming Resistance to Data-Driven Change

1. Identifying Sources of Resistance

- **Common Resistance Factors:** Resistance to data-driven change can stem from various sources, including fear of change, lack of understanding, and perceived threats to job security.

- **Addressing Concerns:** Identify specific concerns and address them through open communication and support. Understanding the root causes of resistance can help in developing effective strategies to overcome it.

2. Communicating the Benefits of Data-Driven Change

- **Highlighting Benefits:** Clearly communicate the benefits of data-driven decision-making to all employees. Emphasize how data can improve business outcomes, enhance efficiency, and contribute to personal and professional growth.
- **Providing Evidence:** Use case studies and examples to demonstrate the positive impact of data-driven decisions. Show how data has led to successful outcomes in other organizations or within your own company.

3. Providing Support and Resources

- **Offering Support:** Provide support to employees during the transition to a data-driven culture. This includes offering guidance, resources, and assistance to help them adapt to new processes and tools.
- **Addressing Skill Gaps:** Identify and address any skill gaps that may be contributing to resistance. Offer additional training and resources to help employees build the necessary skills and confidence.

4. Creating a Safe Environment for Experimentation

- **Encouraging Experimentation:** Foster an environment where experimentation and learning from data are encouraged. Allow employees to test new approaches and learn from their experiences without fear of failure.
- **Learning from Mistakes:** Promote a culture where mistakes are viewed as opportunities for learning and improvement. Encourage employees to

analyze and learn from data-driven decisions that did not achieve the desired outcomes.

5. Building Trust in Data

- **Ensuring Data Accuracy:** Ensure that the data used for decision-making is accurate, reliable, and up-to-date. Address any issues related to data quality and integrity to build trust in the data.
- **Transparency:** Be transparent about how data is collected, analyzed, and used. Providing clarity on data processes can help build trust and reduce resistance.

Practical Steps for Implementing a Data-Driven Culture

1. Assess Current Data Practices

- **Evaluate Existing Practices:** Conduct an assessment of your organization's current data practices and identify areas for improvement. This includes evaluating data collection methods, analysis techniques, and decision-making processes.

2. Develop a Data Strategy

- **Create a Roadmap:** Develop a clear data strategy that outlines your goals, objectives, and the steps needed to build a data-driven culture. This strategy should align with your overall business objectives and provide a roadmap for implementation.

3. Engage Stakeholders

- **Involve Key Stakeholders:** Engage key stakeholders, including leadership, managers, and employees, in the development and implementation of the data strategy. Their input and support are crucial for successful adoption.

4. Monitor Progress and Adjust

- **Track Progress:** Regularly monitor the progress of your data-driven initiatives and assess their impact. Use feedback and performance metrics to make adjustments and improvements as needed.

- **Celebrate Milestones:** Celebrate milestones and achievements related to your data-driven culture. Recognize and reward individuals and teams who contribute to the success of your data initiatives.

5. Continuously Improve

- **Iterative Approach:** Continuously review and refine your data-driven practices. Stay updated on industry trends and best practices to ensure that your data strategy remains relevant and effective.

Building a data-driven culture is a transformative process that requires commitment, education, and ongoing effort. By encouraging a data-driven mindset, training and empowering employees, and overcoming resistance to change, organizations can unlock the full potential of data and drive meaningful improvements in their operations and decision-making. Embracing a data-driven approach not only enhances business performance but also fosters a culture of innovation, collaboration, and continuous improvement. With the right strategies and support, your organization can successfully build a data-driven culture and achieve long-term success.

Chapter Six

Case Studies and Success Stories

1. Success Stories: Entrepreneurs Who Excelled with Data

1.1. Amazon: Revolutionizing Retail with Data

Amazon, founded by Jeff Bezos, is a prime example of a company that has used data to drive its success. From its early days as an online bookstore, Amazon has grown into one of the largest e-commerce platforms globally, thanks in large part to its data-driven approach.

- **Personalization:** Amazon uses data to personalize the shopping experience for each customer. By analyzing browsing history, purchase behavior, and even time spent on various product pages, Amazon recommends products tailored to individual preferences. This personalization has significantly increased conversion rates and customer satisfaction.

- **Inventory Management:** Amazon's data analytics capabilities extend to inventory management. The company uses predictive analytics to forecast demand for products and manage stock levels efficiently. This approach minimizes overstock and stockouts, optimizing inventory turnover and reducing costs.
- **Dynamic Pricing:** Amazon employs dynamic pricing strategies, adjusting prices in real time based on various factors such as demand, competitor pricing, and inventory levels. This data-driven pricing model allows Amazon to remain competitive and maximize revenue.

1.2. Netflix: Transforming Entertainment with Data

Netflix, under the leadership of Reed Hastings, has revolutionized the entertainment industry through its data-driven approach. The company's success can be attributed to its strategic use of data in several key areas:

- **Content Recommendations:** Netflix uses complex algorithms to analyze viewing patterns and preferences. This data enables the platform to recommend content tailored to individual tastes, enhancing user engagement and reducing churn.

- **Original Content Creation:** Netflix leverages data to inform decisions about which original content to produce. By analyzing viewer data and trends, the company identifies content genres and themes with high potential success, guiding its production investments.

- **User Experience Optimization:** Netflix continually analyzes user interactions and feedback to improve the platform's user experience. This data-driven approach helps in refining the interface, improving streaming quality, and enhancing overall customer satisfaction.

1.3. Spotify: Using Data to Drive Music Discovery

Spotify, co-founded by Daniel Ek and Martin Lorentzon, has become a leading music streaming service by leveraging data to enhance user experiences and drive growth.

- **Personalized Playlists:** Spotify's data-driven algorithms create personalized playlists, such as "Discover Weekly" and "Daily Mix," based on users' listening history and preferences. These playlists increase user engagement and encourage continued use of the platform.
- **Artist Insights:** Spotify provides artists with data analytics tools to understand their audience better. By analyzing listener demographics, geographical distribution, and listening habits, artists can tailor their marketing efforts and tour planning.
- **Market Expansion:** Spotify uses data to identify and enter new markets. By analyzing regional listening trends and preferences, Spotify customizes its offerings to cater to local tastes, driving growth in international markets.

2. Lessons Learned from Data-Driven Decision-Making Failures

While data-driven decision-making has proven beneficial for many entrepreneurs, there are notable examples where reliance on data led to failures. Understanding these lessons can help avoid common pitfalls.

2.1. Target's Data Breach and Marketing Misstep

In 2013, Target experienced a massive data breach that exposed customer credit card information. The incident highlighted the risks associated with handling large volumes of sensitive data.

- **Lesson Learned:** Effective data management and security are crucial. Entrepreneurs must invest in robust cybersecurity measures to protect customer data and maintain trust.

2.2. Google Glass: Misinterpreting Market Demand

Google Glass, launched in 2013, was a pioneering wearable technology that ultimately failed to gain widespread adoption. Despite extensive data collection and user testing, Google underestimated privacy concerns and societal readiness for the technology.

- **Lesson Learned:** Data should be complemented with qualitative insights and market research. Entrepreneurs must consider consumer attitudes and societal impacts alongside quantitative data to ensure product viability.

2.3. Quibi: Misjudging Consumer Preferences

Quibi, a short-form video streaming service founded by Jeffrey Katzenberg and Meg Whitman, failed to capture a significant audience despite substantial investments in data and content. The company struggled with high user acquisition costs and an unclear value proposition.

- **Lesson Learned:** Data-driven strategies need to be aligned with a clear understanding of market needs and customer preferences. Entrepreneurs must validate their hypotheses with comprehensive market research and iterative testing.

3. Industry-Specific Case Studies

3.1. E-Commerce: Warby Parker's Data-Driven Approach

Warby Parker, an online eyewear retailer, has effectively used data to disrupt the traditional eyewear industry.

- **Virtual Try-On:** Warby Parker's virtual try-on feature, powered by augmented reality, allows customers to see how different frames look on their faces. This feature was developed based on data analysis of customer preferences and feedback, leading to increased online sales and customer satisfaction.
- **Customer Feedback Integration:** The company actively collects and analyzes customer feedback to improve product offerings and user experience. By using data to address customer concerns and preferences, Warby Parker has built a loyal customer base and enhanced its market position.

3.2. Tech Startups: Airbnb's Use of Data for Growth

Airbnb, founded by Brian Chesky, Joe Gebbia, and Nathan Blecharczyk, has leveraged data to revolutionize the hospitality industry.

- **Dynamic Pricing:** Airbnb uses data to provide hosts with dynamic pricing recommendations. By analyzing factors such as local demand, seasonal trends, and competitor pricing, Airbnb helps hosts optimize their rates and maximize earnings.
- **Trust and Safety:** Data analytics play a critical role in maintaining trust and safety on the platform. Airbnb uses data to detect and prevent fraudulent activity, enhance security measures, and ensure a positive user experience.

3.3. Retail: Walmart's Supply Chain Optimization

Walmart, a retail giant, has long been known for its data-driven approach to supply chain management.

- **Inventory Management:** Walmart's use of real-time data allows the company to optimize inventory levels, manage supplier relationships, and ensure product availability. The company's data-driven supply chain strategies contribute to its competitive pricing and efficient operations.

- **Customer Insights:** Walmart analyzes customer data to personalize marketing efforts and improve product assortments. By understanding purchasing patterns and preferences, Walmart enhances the shopping experience and drives sales.

The use of data-driven decision-making has proven to be a powerful tool for entrepreneurs seeking to enhance their business strategies and drive growth. The success stories of companies like Amazon, Netflix, and Spotify illustrate the transformative impact of data on various aspects of business operations. However, it is essential to learn from failures and challenges, such as Target's data breach and Google Glass's market misjudgment, to avoid common pitfalls.

Industry-specific case studies, including Warby Parker's e-commerce innovations and Airbnb's tech-driven strategies, demonstrate the diverse applications of data in different sectors. By leveraging data effectively, entrepreneurs can make informed decisions, optimize performance, and achieve sustainable success.

Incorporating data into your decision-making processes requires a commitment to continuous learning, adaptation, and a deep understanding of both quantitative and qualitative insights. Embracing a data-driven mindset will empower entrepreneurs to navigate the complexities of the modern business landscape and unlock new opportunities for growth.

Chapter Seven

Challenges and Ethical Considerations

Common Challenges in Data-Driven Decision-Making

1. Data Quality Issues

Accuracy and Reliability: One of the primary challenges in data-driven decision-making is ensuring the accuracy and reliability of the data you use. Data quality issues can arise from various sources, including errors in data entry, outdated information, or inconsistencies across different datasets.

Solutions:

- **Data Validation:** Implement processes for validating and cleansing data before it is used for decision-making. This may involve automated tools for data quality checks and manual review processes.
- **Regular Updates:** Ensure that data is regularly updated to reflect the most current information.

Outdated data can lead to incorrect conclusions and decisions.

- **Data Integration:** Use data integration tools to consolidate data from multiple sources, ensuring consistency and accuracy.

Completeness: Incomplete data can severely impact decision-making. Missing data points can lead to skewed analyses and misguided strategies.

Solutions:

- **Data Collection Strategies:** Develop robust data collection methods to capture all relevant information. This includes setting up comprehensive data entry protocols and using technology to automate data collection.
- **Gap Analysis:** Regularly perform gap analyses to identify and address missing data points. This helps in understanding what data is lacking and why.

2. Analysis Paralysis

Overwhelming Amounts of Data: With the abundance of data available, entrepreneurs often face analysis paralysis—where the sheer volume of data makes it difficult to make decisions. This can lead to delays and indecision.

Solutions:

- **Data Prioritization:** Focus on key metrics and indicators that align with your business goals. Prioritize data that directly impacts decision-making.
- **Data Visualization:** Use data visualization tools to simplify complex data. Charts, graphs, and dashboards can make it easier to interpret data and identify trends.
- **Decision Frameworks:** Implement decision-making frameworks to streamline the process. Frameworks like the RACI matrix (Responsible, Accountable, Consulted, Informed) can help in clarifying roles and responsibilities in decision-making.

Overcomplication: Complicated data models and analyses can obscure insights rather than clarify them. Entrepreneurs may struggle to interpret complex results.

Solutions:

- **Simplified Models:** Use straightforward data models and analyses that are easy to understand. Avoid unnecessary complexity that can hinder decision-making.
- **Clear Communication:** Ensure that data insights are communicated clearly to stakeholders. Provide context and explanations to help others understand the implications of the data.

3. Data Integration Challenges

Siloed Data: Data often resides in separate systems or departments, making it difficult to integrate and analyze comprehensively. Siloed data can lead to incomplete or inconsistent insights.

Solutions:

- **Centralized Data Systems:** Implement centralized data management systems that integrate data from various sources. This allows for a unified view of information.
- **Interoperability:** Ensure that different systems and tools used for data collection and analysis are interoperable. This facilitates smooth data integration and analysis.

Data Compatibility: Different data sources may use varying formats, standards, or terminologies, complicating data integration efforts.

Solutions:

- **Standardization:** Develop and enforce data standards and formats to ensure consistency across different sources. Standardization facilitates easier integration and analysis.
- **Data Transformation Tools:** Utilize data transformation tools to convert data into

compatible formats. This ensures that data from disparate sources can be integrated seamlessly.

Ethical Considerations in Data Use

1. Privacy Concerns

Data Collection: The collection of personal data raises significant privacy concerns. Entrepreneurs must ensure that data collection practices respect individuals' privacy and comply with legal regulations.

Solutions:

- **Transparency:** Clearly communicate to customers what data is being collected and how it will be used. Transparency builds trust and helps in complying with privacy regulations.
- **Consent:** Obtain explicit consent from individuals before collecting their data. This can be done through consent forms or opt-in mechanisms.
- **Data Minimization:** Collect only the data that is necessary for your purposes. Avoid collecting

excessive or irrelevant information that could infringe on privacy.

Data Storage and Security: Storing personal data comes with the responsibility of protecting it from unauthorized access or breaches. Data breaches can have serious repercussions for both individuals and businesses.

Solutions:

- **Data Encryption:** Implement encryption techniques to protect data both in transit and at rest. Encryption ensures that data is secure and inaccessible to unauthorized parties.
- **Access Controls:** Establish strict access controls to limit who can view or manage data. Use authentication and authorization measures to protect sensitive information.
- **Regular Audits:** Conduct regular security audits and vulnerability assessments to identify and address potential risks.

2. Bias and Fairness

Algorithmic Bias: Data-driven decisions are often based on algorithms and models that may inadvertently incorporate biases present in the data. This can lead to unfair or discriminatory outcomes.

Solutions:

- **Bias Detection:** Regularly audit algorithms and data models for bias. Use techniques such as fairness metrics and bias detection tools to identify and mitigate biases.
- **Diverse Data:** Ensure that the data used for training algorithms is diverse and representative. Avoid relying on datasets that may perpetuate existing biases.
- **Inclusive Design:** Design algorithms and data models with inclusivity in mind. Consider the potential impact on different demographic groups and ensure fairness in outcomes.

Decision Transparency: The decision-making process should be transparent to ensure that decisions are based on valid and ethical criteria.

Solutions:

- **Explainability:** Use explainable AI techniques to make algorithms and models more transparent. Provide explanations for how decisions are made and the factors considered.
- **Documentation:** Maintain detailed documentation of data sources, algorithms, and decision-making processes. This helps in ensuring accountability and transparency.

3. Ethical Use of Data

Purpose Limitation: Data should be used only for the purposes for which it was collected. Using data for unintended purposes can raise ethical concerns and violate trust.

Solutions:

- **Purpose Specification:** Clearly define the purpose of data collection and use. Ensure that data is used in accordance with the specified purpose.
- **Ethical Guidelines:** Develop and adhere to ethical guidelines for data use. Establish policies and procedures to ensure that data is used responsibly.

Data Ownership: Ownership and control of data can be contentious, especially when dealing with third-party data sources or user-generated content.

Solutions:

- **Clear Agreements:** Establish clear agreements and contracts regarding data ownership and usage rights. Ensure that all parties involved understand and agree to the terms.
- **User Rights:** Respect users' rights to access, correct, or delete their data. Provide mechanisms

for users to exercise control over their personal information.

Navigating Challenges and Ethical Considerations

1. Establish a Data Governance Framework

Governance Structure: Implement a data governance framework to manage data quality, privacy, and ethical use. This includes defining roles and responsibilities for data management and decision-making.

Components:

- **Data Stewards:** Designate individuals or teams responsible for overseeing data quality and compliance.
- **Policies and Procedures:** Develop and enforce policies and procedures for data management, security, and ethical use.
- **Training:** Provide training for employees on data governance, privacy, and ethical considerations.

2. Foster a Culture of Data Responsibility

Awareness and Education: Promote awareness and education about data challenges and ethical considerations within your organization. Ensure that all employees understand the importance of data quality and ethical use.

Strategies:

- **Workshops and Seminars:** Conduct workshops and seminars on data governance and ethical considerations.
- **Ongoing Training:** Offer ongoing training and resources to keep employees informed about best practices and regulatory changes.

3. Implement Robust Data Management Practices

Data Quality Management: Adopt best practices for data quality management to address issues related to accuracy, completeness, and consistency.

Practices:

- **Data Audits:** Regularly perform data audits to identify and address quality issues.
- **Data Integration:** Ensure seamless integration of data from different sources to maintain consistency and accuracy.

4. Embrace Transparency and Accountability

Open Communication: Communicate openly with stakeholders about data practices, including data collection methods, usage, and security measures.

Actions:

- **Transparency Reports:** Publish transparency reports detailing data practices and governance measures.
- **Stakeholder Engagement:** Engage with stakeholders to address concerns and gather feedback on data practices.

5. Stay Informed and Adapt

Regulatory Changes: Stay informed about changes in data protection regulations and industry standards. Adapt your data practices to comply with new requirements.

Actions:

- **Legal Consultation:** Consult legal experts to ensure compliance with data protection laws and regulations.
- **Industry Trends:** Monitor industry trends and best practices to stay ahead of emerging challenges and opportunities.

Navigating the challenges and ethical considerations of data-driven decision-making requires a thoughtful approach and a commitment to best practices. By addressing issues related to data quality, analysis paralysis, privacy, bias, and ethical use, entrepreneurs can make informed decisions that drive business success while maintaining trust and integrity. Implementing robust data management practices, fostering a culture of responsibility, and staying informed about regulatory changes are key to overcoming these challenges and ensuring that data is used effectively and ethically.

Chapter Eight

Implementing Data-Driven Decisions

1. Steps for Making Data-Driven Decisions

1.1 Identifying Objectives and Key Questions

Before diving into data collection, clearly define the objectives you aim to achieve and the key questions you need to answer. Objectives might include increasing sales, improving customer retention, or optimizing operational efficiency. Key questions could be:

- What factors are driving our sales growth?
- How can we reduce customer churn?
- What operational inefficiencies are affecting our profit margins?

1.2 Collecting Relevant Data

1.2.1 Data Sources

Identify and gather data from various sources relevant to your business objectives. Common sources include:

- **Customer Data:** Purchase history, demographics, feedback, and behavior patterns.
- **Sales Data:** Revenue, order volume, average order value, and sales by product or region.
- **Marketing Data:** Campaign performance, conversion rates, traffic sources, and customer engagement metrics.
- **Operational Data:** Inventory levels, supply chain metrics, and production costs.

1.2.2 Data Collection Methods

Utilize a range of methods to collect data, such as:

- **Surveys and Feedback Forms:** Directly gather customer opinions and feedback.
- **Web Analytics:** Tools like Google Analytics to track website traffic, user behavior, and conversion rates.
- **CRM Systems:** Track customer interactions, sales activities, and support requests.

- **Sales and Financial Reports:** Analyze historical sales data and financial performance.

1.2.3 Ensuring Data Quality

Ensure the data collected is accurate, complete, and reliable. Steps to maintain data quality include:

- **Validation:** Cross-check data against known sources or benchmarks.
- **Cleaning:** Remove duplicates, correct errors, and fill in missing values.
- **Consistency:** Ensure data is recorded in a uniform format and adheres to standards.

1.3 Analyzing Data

1.3.1 Data Analysis Techniques

Use various techniques to analyze the data:

- **Descriptive Analysis:** Summarize and describe the main features of the dataset (e.g., averages, percentages).

- **Diagnostic Analysis:** Identify patterns or reasons behind trends (e.g., why sales increased in a particular region).
- **Predictive Analysis:** Forecast future trends based on historical data (e.g., sales predictions using regression models).
- **Prescriptive Analysis:** Recommend actions based on data insights (e.g., optimizing marketing strategies based on performance data).

1.3.2 Data Visualization

Visualize data to make complex information more comprehensible. Tools for data visualization include:

- **Charts and Graphs:** Bar charts, line graphs, and pie charts to represent data trends and comparisons.
- **Dashboards:** Interactive dashboards for real-time monitoring of key metrics.
- **Heatmaps:** Visualize user interactions on websites or apps to identify high and low engagement areas.

1.4 Making Decisions

Based on the data analysis, make informed decisions that align with your objectives. Consider:

- **Data Insights:** What do the data trends and patterns suggest?
- **Potential Actions:** What actions can address the identified issues or leverage opportunities?
- **Risk Assessment:** What are the potential risks associated with the proposed actions?

1.5 Implementing Decisions

Execute the chosen strategies with a clear plan:

- **Action Plan:** Develop a detailed plan outlining the steps required to implement the decision.
- **Resource Allocation:** Allocate the necessary resources, including personnel, budget, and technology.
- **Communication:** Communicate the changes to relevant stakeholders and ensure they understand their roles in the implementation process.

2. Monitoring and Evaluating the Outcomes of Data-Driven Strategies

2.1 Setting Up Monitoring Systems

2.1.1 Define Key Metrics

Establish key performance indicators (KPIs) that align with your objectives and will help track the success of your data-driven strategies. Examples include:

- **Sales Growth:** Measure the increase in sales revenue.
- **Customer Retention Rate:** Track the percentage of customers who return.
- **Operational Efficiency:** Monitor improvements in production or supply chain processes.

2.1.2 Implement Tracking Tools

Use tracking tools to monitor performance:

- **Performance Dashboards:** Real-time dashboards to track KPIs and other important metrics.
- **Automated Reports:** Set up automated reports to regularly review data and performance indicators.

- **Alerts and Notifications:** Configure alerts for significant changes or deviations from expected performance.

2.2 Evaluating Outcomes

2.2.1 Comparing Results Against Objectives

Assess whether the implemented strategies have achieved the desired outcomes. Compare actual results with the objectives and benchmarks established earlier:

- **Success Evaluation:** Determine if the objectives have been met or exceeded.
- **Gap Analysis:** Identify any discrepancies between expected and actual results.

2.2.2 Analyzing Performance Trends

Review performance trends over time to understand the long-term impact of the strategies:

- **Trend Analysis:** Analyze data trends to identify patterns or shifts in performance.

- **Segment Analysis:** Break down performance data by segments (e.g., customer demographics, product categories) to gain deeper insights.

2.2.3 Feedback Collection

Collect feedback from stakeholders and customers to gain additional perspectives:

- **Employee Feedback:** Gather input from employees involved in the implementation process to understand any operational challenges.
- **Customer Feedback:** Solicit feedback from customers to assess their satisfaction and the effectiveness of changes made.

2.3 Reporting and Communication

2.3.1 Preparing Reports

Compile detailed reports summarizing the outcomes of data-driven strategies:

- **Executive Summary:** Provide a high-level overview of results and key insights.

- **Detailed Analysis:** Include detailed findings, trends, and comparisons with objectives.
- **Visual Representations:** Use charts, graphs, and tables to present data clearly.

2.3.2 Communicating Results

Share the results with relevant stakeholders:

- **Internal Communication:** Present findings to team members, managers, and executives.
- **External Communication:** Share relevant insights with customers or partners if appropriate.

3. Iterating and Improving Based on Results

3.1 Identifying Areas for Improvement

Based on the evaluation of outcomes, identify areas where further improvements are needed:

- **Performance Gaps:** Determine areas where results fell short of expectations.
- **Inefficiencies:** Identify any operational or strategic inefficiencies.

- **Opportunities:** Look for new opportunities to capitalize on based on data insights.

3.2 Developing Improvement Plans

3.2.1 Refining Strategies

Adjust existing strategies based on the insights gained:

- **Strategy Revision:** Modify strategies to address performance gaps or capitalize on new opportunities.
- **Optimization:** Implement improvements to optimize processes, marketing, or product offerings.

3.2.2 Testing New Approaches

Test new approaches to validate their effectiveness:

- **Pilot Programs:** Run pilot programs to test new strategies on a smaller scale before full implementation.

- **A/B Testing:** Conduct A/B tests to compare different versions of strategies and determine the most effective approach.

3.3 Implementing Improvements

Execute the refined strategies and improvements with a clear plan:

- **Action Plan:** Develop and implement a new action plan for the revised strategies.
- **Resource Allocation:** Allocate resources as needed for the new or adjusted strategies.
- **Monitoring:** Continue monitoring performance to ensure the improvements are achieving the desired outcomes.

3.4 Continuous Learning and Adaptation

Foster a culture of continuous learning and adaptation:

- **Feedback Loops:** Establish mechanisms for ongoing feedback from employees and customers.

- **Regular Reviews:** Conduct regular reviews of data and performance to stay aligned with evolving business goals.
- **Learning and Development:** Invest in learning and development to keep up with industry trends and best practices.

Implementing data-driven decisions is a dynamic and ongoing process that involves careful planning, execution, and continuous improvement. By following a structured approach—from collecting and analyzing data to monitoring outcomes and iterating based on results—you can make informed decisions that drive business success. Embracing a data-driven mindset enables entrepreneurs to leverage insights, optimize strategies, and achieve sustainable growth in a competitive landscape.

Chapter Nine

The Future of Data-Driven Decision-Making

Emerging Trends in Data Analytics and AI

1. Advanced Predictive Analytics

Predictive analytics involves using historical data to forecast future outcomes. Recent advancements in predictive analytics are increasingly sophisticated, leveraging machine learning (ML) and AI algorithms to improve accuracy and uncover deeper insights. These advanced tools analyze vast amounts of data to identify patterns and predict future trends with greater precision.

- **Real-Time Data Processing:** Traditional predictive analytics often relied on batch processing, which could delay insights. Real-time data processing allows businesses to make decisions based on the most current information, improving responsiveness and agility.

- **Enhanced Algorithms:** Newer algorithms, such as ensemble methods and deep learning models, offer improved prediction accuracy by combining multiple models or simulating complex neural networks.

2. AI-Powered Decision Support Systems

AI-powered decision support systems are transforming how entrepreneurs make strategic decisions. These systems integrate AI and data analytics to provide actionable recommendations and insights.

- **Automated Decision-Making:** AI systems can automate routine decision-making processes, freeing up time for entrepreneurs to focus on more strategic tasks. For example, AI can optimize inventory levels, pricing strategies, and marketing campaigns based on real-time data.
- **Augmented Intelligence:** Rather than replacing human decision-makers, AI augments their capabilities by providing data-driven insights and recommendations. This partnership between

human and machine can lead to more informed and strategic decisions.

3. Enhanced Data Visualization

Data visualization has evolved from static charts and graphs to interactive and immersive tools that help users explore and understand complex data sets.

- **Interactive Dashboards:** Modern data visualization tools offer interactive dashboards that allow users to drill down into data, explore various scenarios, and visualize trends in real-time.
- **Augmented Reality (AR) and Virtual Reality (VR):** AR and VR technologies are beginning to be used for data visualization, providing immersive experiences that help users better understand and analyze data.

4. Data Privacy and Ethics

As data collection and analysis become more pervasive, data privacy and ethical considerations are gaining prominence. Emerging trends focus on ensuring that data practices are transparent and respectful of user privacy.

- **Regulatory Compliance:** With regulations such as GDPR and CCPA, businesses need to ensure compliance with data protection laws. Future trends will likely involve more stringent regulations and greater emphasis on data stewardship.
- **Ethical AI:** There is a growing focus on ethical AI practices, including addressing biases in algorithms and ensuring that AI systems are used responsibly.

5. Integration of IoT and Data Analytics

The Internet of Things (IoT) involves connecting physical devices to the internet, allowing them to collect and share data. The integration of IoT with data analytics is providing new opportunities for businesses to gain insights and optimize operations.

- **Smart Devices:** IoT devices, such as sensors and wearables, generate vast amounts of data that can be analyzed to improve processes, enhance customer experiences, and make data-driven decisions.
- **Predictive Maintenance:** IoT data can be used for predictive maintenance, anticipating equipment failures before they occur and minimizing downtime.

How Future Technologies Will Impact Decision-Making for Entrepreneurs

1. The Rise of Autonomous Systems

Autonomous systems, powered by AI and robotics, are set to impact various aspects of business operations.

- **Self-Driving Vehicles:** Autonomous vehicles can transform logistics and supply chain management by reducing transportation costs and improving efficiency. Businesses will need to adapt to changes in shipping and delivery processes.

- **Robotic Process Automation (RPA):** RPA uses robots to automate repetitive tasks, such as data entry and customer service. Entrepreneurs can leverage RPA to streamline operations and reduce manual errors.

2. Advanced AI Algorithms

Future AI algorithms will continue to evolve, offering even more sophisticated insights and capabilities.

- **Explainable AI:** As AI systems become more complex, there is a growing need for explainable AI, which provides transparency into how decisions are made. This will help businesses understand AI-driven recommendations and build trust in the technology.
- **Cognitive Computing:** Cognitive computing aims to simulate human thought processes and decision-making. This technology will enhance AI's ability to understand context, interpret complex data, and provide nuanced insights.

3. Blockchain for Data Security

Blockchain technology, known for its role in cryptocurrency, offers potential benefits for data security and transparency.

- **Immutable Records:** Blockchain creates immutable records of transactions and data exchanges, enhancing data integrity and reducing the risk of tampering.
- **Decentralized Data Storage:** Blockchain enables decentralized data storage, which can enhance security and reduce reliance on central data repositories.

4. Enhanced Personalization

Future technologies will enable even more personalized experiences for customers.

- **AI-Driven Personalization:** AI algorithms will continue to refine personalization by analyzing user behavior and preferences to deliver tailored recommendations and experiences.

- **Dynamic Pricing:** Advanced analytics will allow businesses to implement dynamic pricing strategies based on real-time demand, competitor pricing, and customer behavior.

5. Improved Collaboration Tools

Future technologies will enhance collaboration and communication within organizations.

- **AI-Powered Collaboration Platforms:** AI will improve collaboration tools by automating scheduling, managing tasks, and facilitating communication between team members.
- **Virtual Workspaces:** Virtual reality and augmented reality will provide immersive virtual workspaces, enabling remote teams to collaborate more effectively.

Preparing Your Business for a Data-Driven Future

1. Investing in Technology and Skills

To thrive in a data-driven future, businesses need to invest in the right technologies and skills.

- **Technology Investments:** Invest in data analytics platforms, AI tools, and data visualization software to leverage the latest advancements in technology.
- **Skills Development:** Train your team in data analysis, AI technologies, and data privacy to ensure they have the skills needed to navigate a data-driven environment.

2. Building a Data-Driven Culture

Creating a culture that values data-driven decision-making is essential for long-term success.

- **Promoting Data Literacy:** Encourage employees to develop data literacy skills and understand the importance of data in decision-making.
- **Data-Driven Decision-Making:** Foster an environment where decisions are based on data insights rather than intuition or assumptions.

3. Establishing Data Governance and Privacy Practices

Proper data governance and privacy practices are crucial for maintaining trust and compliance.

- **Data Governance Framework:** Implement a data governance framework to manage data quality, security, and compliance.
- **Privacy Policies:** Develop and enforce privacy policies that adhere to regulations and ensure the ethical use of data.

4. Embracing Innovation

Stay ahead of the curve by embracing innovation and adapting to emerging technologies.

- **Continuous Learning:** Keep up with industry trends and technological advancements through continuous learning and professional development.
- **Pilot Programs:** Experiment with new technologies and approaches through pilot programs to

evaluate their impact before full-scale implementation.

5. Building Strategic Partnerships

Form strategic partnerships with technology providers and industry experts to access the latest tools and insights.

- **Technology Partners:** Collaborate with technology vendors and consultants to implement and optimize data-driven solutions.
- **Industry Networks:** Join industry networks and forums to share knowledge, learn from peers, and stay informed about best practices.

The future of data-driven decision-making is filled with opportunities and challenges as emerging trends in data analytics and AI continue to evolve. Entrepreneurs who embrace these technologies and prepare their businesses for a data-driven future will be better positioned to make informed decisions, optimize operations, and drive growth. By investing in technology, building a data-driven culture, and staying ahead of trends, businesses can harness the power of data to achieve long-term success and maintain a competitive edge in an increasingly data-centric world.

Chapter Ten

Conclusion

Recap of Key Points

1. The Importance of Data-Driven Decision-Making

Data-driven decision-making (DDDM) involves using data as a fundamental input in the decision-making process. Unlike intuition-based decisions, which rely on personal judgment and experience, data-driven decisions are grounded in empirical evidence and statistical analysis. This approach offers several advantages:

- **Objective Insights:** Data provides an objective foundation for decisions, reducing the influence of personal biases and subjective opinions.
- **Improved Accuracy:** Decisions based on data are generally more accurate because they reflect real-world trends and patterns.

- **Enhanced Strategic Planning:** Data enables entrepreneurs to identify market trends, customer preferences, and competitive dynamics, leading to more effective strategic planning.

2. Collecting and Analyzing Data

Successful data-driven decision-making begins with robust data collection and analysis:

- **Types of Data:** Entrepreneurs need to understand different types of data, such as quantitative (numerical) and qualitative (descriptive). Quantitative data includes metrics like sales figures and website traffic, while qualitative data involves insights from customer feedback and market research.
- **Data Sources:** Key sources include customer interactions, sales data, market research reports, and social media analytics. Each source provides unique insights that contribute to a comprehensive understanding of business performance.

- **Tools and Technologies:** Leveraging advanced tools like Google Analytics, CRM systems, and data visualization platforms helps in efficient data collection and analysis. These tools transform raw data into actionable insights.

3. Integrating Data into Business Strategy

Integrating data into your business strategy involves:

- **Aligning Insights with Goals:** Use data to inform strategic goals and objectives. For example, data on customer behavior can guide marketing strategies, while sales data can influence product development.
- **Identifying Opportunities and Risks:** Data helps in spotting market opportunities and potential risks. For instance, analyzing customer feedback can reveal unmet needs, while tracking sales trends can highlight declining product performance.

- **Making Informed Decisions:** Data-driven insights should guide critical business decisions, from marketing campaigns to product launches and operational improvements.

4. Building a Data-Driven Culture

Creating a culture that values data involves:

- **Encouraging a Data-Driven Mindset:** Promote the use of data in everyday decision-making. Encourage team members to rely on data rather than intuition when evaluating performance and making decisions.
- **Training and Development:** Invest in training programs to enhance data literacy among employees. Equip your team with the skills needed to analyze and interpret data effectively.
- **Overcoming Resistance:** Address any resistance to data-driven change by demonstrating the value of data and providing support for those adapting to new practices.

5. Overcoming Challenges and Ethical Considerations

Data-driven decision-making is not without its challenges:

- **Data Quality:** Ensure data accuracy and reliability. Poor-quality data can lead to incorrect conclusions and ineffective strategies.
- **Analysis Paralysis:** Avoid becoming overwhelmed by data. Focus on the most relevant metrics and insights to make clear, actionable decisions.
- **Ethical Considerations:** Address ethical issues such as data privacy and bias. Ensure that data collection and usage comply with legal standards and ethical guidelines.

6. Implementing and Monitoring Data-Driven Decisions

Effective implementation involves:

- **Execution:** Translate data insights into actionable strategies and initiatives. For example, if data reveals a gap in customer satisfaction, implement targeted improvements in customer service.

- **Monitoring:** Regularly review the outcomes of data-driven decisions to assess their effectiveness. Use performance metrics to track progress and make necessary adjustments.
- **Iteration:** Continuously refine strategies based on feedback and new data. The iterative process ensures that decisions remain relevant and effective over time.

Encouragement for Entrepreneurs to Embrace Data in Their Decision-Making Processes

As an entrepreneur, embracing data-driven decision-making can transform the way you operate your business. Here's why you should consider making data a core part of your decision-making process:

- **Enhanced Decision Quality:** Data provides a clearer picture of market dynamics, customer preferences, and operational performance. This clarity leads to better-informed decisions that are more likely to yield positive outcomes.

- **Increased Efficiency:** Data-driven insights help streamline operations by identifying inefficiencies and areas for improvement. This efficiency translates into cost savings and increased productivity.
- **Competitive Advantage:** Utilizing data effectively can give you a competitive edge. By understanding market trends and customer behavior, you can anticipate changes and stay ahead of competitors.
- **Strategic Growth:** Data enables strategic planning and forecasting. With accurate insights, you can make informed decisions about scaling your business, entering new markets, and investing in innovation.

To fully leverage data, it's essential to cultivate a mindset that values empirical evidence and analytical thinking. This shift in approach requires commitment and an openness to change, but the benefits are well worth the effort.

Next Steps and Resources for Further Learning

To continue your journey toward becoming a data-driven entrepreneur, consider the following steps and resources:

1. Develop Your Data Literacy

- **Online Courses:** Enroll in online courses focused on data analytics, data science, and data visualization. Platforms like Coursera, edX, and Udacity offer courses designed for various skill levels.
- **Books and Guides:** Read books such as *"Data-Driven: Creating a Data Culture"* by Hilary Mason and DJ Patil, and *"The Data Warehouse Toolkit"* by Ralph Kimball and Margy Ross. These resources provide foundational knowledge and practical insights into data-driven decision-making.

2. Utilize Data Analytics Tools

- **Google Analytics:** Explore Google Analytics tutorials and resources to learn how to effectively use the platform for tracking website performance and user behavior.
- **CRM Systems:** Familiarize yourself with CRM systems like Salesforce or HubSpot. These tools offer insights into customer interactions and sales data.

3. Build and Analyze Your Data

- **Data Collection:** Start by collecting data relevant to your business. Set up systems for tracking key metrics and ensuring data accuracy.
- **Data Analysis:** Practice analyzing data using tools like Excel, Tableau, or Power BI. Develop skills in data visualization and interpretation to make informed decisions.

4. Engage with Data Communities

- **Networking:** Join data analytics and business intelligence communities. Engage with professionals in forums, LinkedIn groups, and local meetups to exchange ideas and stay updated on industry trends.
- **Conferences and Workshops:** Attend conferences and workshops focused on data science and analytics. These events provide opportunities to learn from experts and network with peers.

5. Implement and Iterate

- **Pilot Projects:** Test data-driven strategies on a small scale before full implementation. Use these pilot projects to refine your approach and measure effectiveness.
- **Feedback and Improvement:** Continuously seek feedback from your team and stakeholders. Use this feedback to make iterative improvements to your data-driven practices.

6. Stay Informed

- **Industry Trends:** Keep up with emerging trends in data analytics, such as advancements in artificial intelligence and machine learning. Staying informed helps you adapt to new technologies and maintain a competitive edge.
- **Ongoing Learning:** Commit to ongoing learning and professional development. The field of data analytics is constantly evolving, and staying current ensures that your skills and knowledge remain relevant.

By taking these steps, you can build a strong foundation in data-driven decision-making and harness the power of data to drive your business success. Embrace data as a valuable asset, and let it guide you toward informed, strategic decisions that propel your entrepreneurial journey forward.

In summary, data-driven decision-making is a transformative approach that empowers entrepreneurs to make informed, strategic choices based on empirical evidence. By understanding the importance of data, mastering data collection and analysis, and building a culture that values data, you can enhance your business operations, achieve better outcomes, and gain a competitive advantage. Embrace the principles of data-driven decision-making, invest in your data literacy, and leverage the tools and resources available to continue learning and growing. With a data-driven mindset, you're well-equipped to navigate the complexities of entrepreneurship and drive your business toward sustained success.

www.ingramcontent.com/pod-product-compliance
Lightning Source LLC
Chambersburg PA
CBHW082235220526
45479CB00005B/1245